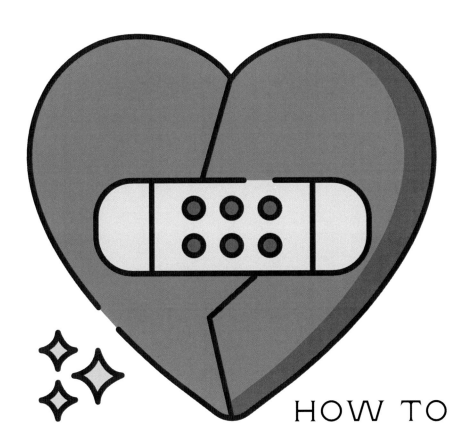

HOW TO

THE FORMULA FOR LIFE
A Universal Guide

DAISY PAPP

HOW TO
5+2

CONTENT

FOLLOW

facebook.com/daisy.papp
instagram.com/daisypapp
twitter.com/DaisyPapp

HOW TO
5+2

WHAT IS IN THIS BOOK

1
CONSIDERATION

2
ADMIRATION

3
RESPECT

4
EMPATHY

5
DIGNITY

6
TIPS, TOOLS, SKILLS

7
THE +2

8
WHO AM I TO
WRITE THIS BOOK?

9
THANK YOU

MY MESSAGE
TO YOU

DEDICATION

To all the children and teenagers in this world including future generations. It is my passion to share with you all I needed to know when I was your age. When you love your heart and protect it as you wished your biggest hero would protect you, then you become the hero for your heart and to yourself. You are loved. You are worthy! You are a marvel! You are talented! You have so many gifts to bring into this world!

FOREWORD

What a great honor and also challenge it is to write to you, young humans. My name is Daisy Papp and it has been a while since I was your age. All I can tell you is that it is worthwhile to look at the many wonders in life. Is it always going to be easy? Not really. I admit that challenges are part of life and they are opportunities to grow and evolve at the same time.

I wish that I could prevent you from future tests and past sadness but that is not possible. My promise to you is that I do my best and give you hints, tools, and knowledge that work for me. All of what you can find on the following pages I wish I had known when I was your age. Well, that was not the case. Nevertheless, **today** I am grateful to know what I do know and that I can share with you my humble knowledge. Thank you for reading my words!

WHAT IS THIS BOOK ABOUT?

This book is divided into chapters. Every chapter begins with the definition of each of the **5+2** points. I share with you what I have learned and what works for me and thousands of people around the world. I live by the **5+2** principle and formula. The result is that I am equipped for life, and you can be too. Most importantly, you learn how to be your own best friend. Think you can't do that? I will do my best to make it easy and fun. It will be my pleasure to hear from you and learn from you how I can make this book even better for you and other humans your age. All humans are educators and students at the same time. Remember, not one human is smart enough to know it all, and no one is stupid enough to never be right. Enjoy my words and I assure you that I speak from my heart to yours.

You can go directly to the 5+2 definitions and skip the following few pages and come back later when you feel like it. Either way you invest in yourself. Investing in yourself is the best investment you can ever make.

Let's clarify one important fact first:

What makes a human is how he/she behaves. People are **not** what they look like or what they say or own. This also means that you are **not** what you look like or what you say or own. What makes you is how you behave! Behavior is always a choice.

How you look
is not
who you are!

• • • • • • • • • • • • • • • • • • •

When you arrived into this world (at birth) the adults in your environment had already lived for years and had good and bad experiences.

The people in your environment:
- got hurt
- had fears
- accomplished goals
- had fun and joy
- were upset at times
- cried tears
- had new friends
- were happy
- got disappointed, and much more

Whatever happened before you were born has nothing to do with you. It has to do with the lives of your ancestors: The lives of your parents, your grandparents, your great grandparents and so forth. Their experiences happened in **their** lives. It is like a backpack in which the experiences and the connected feelings and emotions are stored. Emotions happen in the body. Emotion is easy to remember:
E-motion >>> Energy in motion.

The emotional backpack of the adults, parents, care-takers and older siblings was already filled with stuff before you arrived into this world.

Emotional backpack

You learn everything from the young and old people surrounding you. The humans around you do their best and give you what they have learned during their lives, the good and not so good alike. They only know what they have received from their ancestors and people surrounding them when they arrived into this world plus what they learned through life. That is what they pass on.

EARLY BABY DEVELOPMENT

Usually when you started to crawl and also when you took your first steps to discover the world much encouragement happened to keep you going and growing.

YOU CAN
DO iT

The mumbling of your first words were awesome and also encouraged. But then something really weird happened...

When you finally started speaking you oftentimes were told to be quiet.

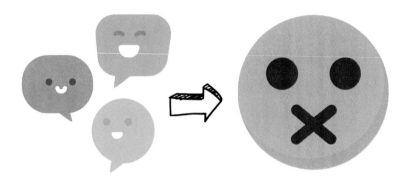

Something similar happened with walking: Ideally you were encouraged to take your first steps and once you had the courage to investigate the world around you the adults or older siblings wanted you to stay and not walk and explore. This is very confusing. Do you agree?

By the time you are the age to visit Kindergarten or Pre-School things have changed from the first encouragements after birth to the following:

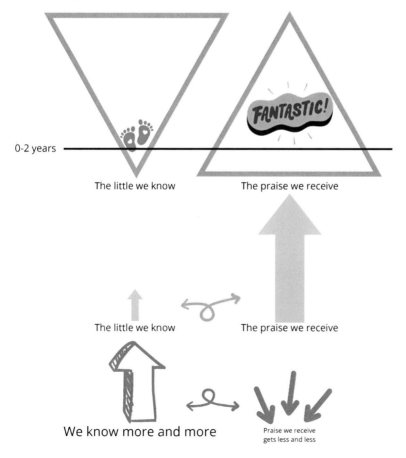

13

~Note: Invitation to think for a moment~

"What is my purpose in life?" I asked myself.

"What if I told you that you fulfilled your purpose when you took an extra moment to talk to that kid about his life?" told a voice.

"Or when you helped picking up the bag when your neighbor dropped it? Or when you saved that dog from walking on the street into traffic? Or when you tied your grandparent's shoes for them?"

"The problem is when you equate your purpose with goal-based achievement. The Universe is not interested in your achievements. The Universe is interested in your heart. When you choose to act out of kindness, passion and love, you are already aligned with your purpose.
No need to look any further."

There are many rules you learned since you were born. Not all families, all schools, all communities have the same rules, sadly, so I think when we look at <u>basic rules</u>. Basic rules are something like the FIFA (*Féderacion Internationale de football association*) applies to all soccer games around the world. When the greatest soccer players in the world play a match they play by the same rules as players at the little club in a small town.

The tennis rules are also the same in all tennis clubs around the world.

When we look at families the basic rules vary. Imagine a world where the following 5 points of the 5+2 were standard: Consideration, admiration, respect, empathy, dignity.

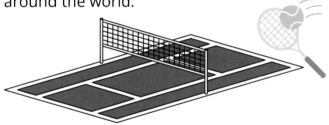

I like the play on words: Standard = the art of standing. The 5+2 formula as a standard helps to stand well in life.

I cannot change the rules in any family but only in my own family. So, it is up to you to find healthy rules you can develop, adopt and apply. It is possible to inspire others when you lead by example and live by these basic rules.

It is my wish to inspire all the people around the world to be inspired and adopt these simple basic rules.

The 5+2 formula has been applied in many families, communities, and businesses for over 12 years. The wonderful results repoerted by people from around the world speak for themselves. Let's have a closer look at the 5+2 in the following chapters.

1.

CONSIDERATION

1.

con·sid·er·a·tion
kən͵sidər'āSH(ə)n/

noun

Thinking carefully about something is like taking your time to decide. It's like when you choose what game to play or take an extra moment to think about what snack to eat. Before making a decision it is good to think about it. When you really think about things, it's like having a special time in your head to decide what's best. You might think about the fun and the not-so-fun sides of your decision before you make it.

Thinking carefully also means considering how your choices might impact others or make others feel. You want to make choices that don't hurt or upset anyone. It also means that you take your time to think how you will feel about your choices later. Sometimes, you think about what will happen next if you choose one thing over another. It is like a meeting between your head and your heart, where you consider all the possibilities before making a choice or decision. That's how to be a wise decision maker!

Examples:

Consideration means thinking about how others feel and treating them nicely. Here are some examples:

- Imagine how you would feel if you were in someone else's shoes. Try to understand their feelings and be kind.
- Show thoughtfulness, kindness, and good manners when you interact with others. A friendly "please" and "thank you" can go a long way.
- Be interested in what others have to say and treat them with respect. Everyone is different, and that's okay!
- Don't treat people unfairly because of their culture, beliefs, or the way they look or think. Treat everyone equally.
- Respect other people's things just like you want them to respect yours.
- Consider how others might be feeling physically and emotionally. Be understanding and caring.
- Be considerate to yourself too! Take care of your own feelings and needs.

How you treat others is a reflection of your relationship with yourself. When you are kind and compassionate to yourself you will be more likely to be kind and considerate to others. When you are kind to others they will likely reflect that back to you.

Here's another example: If you know someone is trying not to eat sweets, don't eat candy in front of them or give them candy. That is being considerate of their feelings and choices. When you don't want to eat sweets and other's offer you or eat sweets in front of you, you can kindly ask them to be considerate. In this example, you can also be considerate of yourself by leaving the room if someone is eating candy in front of you when you don't want to eat candy yourself right now.

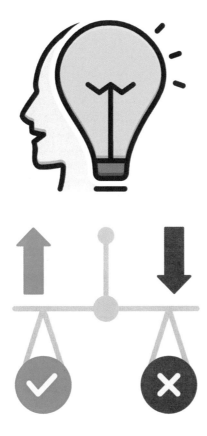

2.

ADMIRATION

2.

ad·mi·ra·tion

admə'rāSH(ə)n/

noun

Admiration means feeling happy and liking something or someone. It's like clapping and saying nice things to show that you really like what someone did.

When you give compliments, it's like saying kind and positive words to express your admiration. It's also like thinking about something or someone and feeling really happy about it.

Examples:
Admiration means acknowledging and enjoying other people's qualities and feeling inspired to develop those qualities in yourself. Here are some examples:

- Admiration is a feeling we have when we really like and look up to someone or something. It's like having a superhero or a role model that you think is amazing and want to be like.

- For example, if you admire a famous athlete, you think they are incredibly talented and you might want to play sports just like them when you grow up. Or if you admire a teacher, you think he or she is very smart and kind, so you might want to be an especially good student.
- Admiration is when you feel a lot of respect and inspiration for someone because of their special qualities or talents. It's like having a big "Wow!" feeling about them in your heart because they are so impressive to you. And it's okay to have many different people or things that you admire in life.
- Remember, admiration is a positive feeling, and it can be a great source of inspiration for you to become the best version of yourself!

3.

RESPECT

3.

re·spect
rəˈspekt/

noun

Respect means thinking that someone or something is great, valuable and important. It's like understanding that people and things are serious and should be treated with kindness and good manners. It's also like having a special way of thinking or looking at someone or something in a nice and considerate way.

Examples:
Understanding *respect* can be simple and easy. Here's how you can learn to understand it:

- Respect means treating others the way you want to be treated. It's like being kind and polite to everyone, like your friends, family, teachers, and even people you just met. When you show respect, you use good manners like a simple "please" and "thank you." You also listen to what others have to say and wait for your turn to talk.

- Respecting someone's feelings means being careful with your words and not saying mean things that could hurt them. It's important to remember that everyone is different, and we can be nice and understanding even if we don't agree with them or don't like the same things they do.
- You can show respect by being helpful and sharing with others. If someone needs help or is feeling sad, you can offer to help them or be there to comfort them. Treating other people's things with care is also a way to show respect.
- Remember, when you treat others with respect, they will be happy to be around you. And they may also show respect to you. It's like spreading kindness and making the world a better place!

4.

EMPATHY

4.

em·pa·thy
ˈempəTHē/

noun

Seeing from the other human's point of view and being interested in their feelings as well. Empathy means putting yourself in someone else's shoes, seeing from the other human's point of view, care and being interested in their feelings as well. It's like understanding and relating to how someone else is feeling and what they are going through. Empathy is when you act with a caring and loving attitude towards others, like being kind and helpful. It's like trying to understand and imagine how someone else feels and seeing things from their point of view.

Empathy helps us understand that every human has their own inner world. We cannot know what goes on in anybody's inner world and what causes challenges in their lives. Our empathy can shine a light from our heart and may inspire others to be empathetic too.

Examples:

Empathy is when you try to understand how someone else is feeling and share those feelings with them. For example, if your friend is sad because they lost a game. Empathy is when you feel for them and try to comfort them. It's like being a good friend and being there for them when they need you.

- Empathy helps us be kind and caring towards others.
- It's like putting yourself in other's shoes and caring about how they feel.
- When we have empathy, we can imagine how others are feeling, and that helps us treat them with kindness and love.
- It's like having a special superpower that helps us be better friends and make the world a happier place!

It is also important that you have empathy for yourself. There is a big difference between pity and empathy, self-pity and self-empathy. Self-empathy is healthy and very important to live a contented life.

5.

DIGNITY

5.
dig·ni·ty
ˈdignədē/
noun

Dignity means being worthy of honor and respect. Everyone is worthy of dignity. Wherever you are born, whenever you are born, dignity is not about looks or grades. Dignity is like having a special kind of greatness inside you. It's like having a positive attitude and behaving in a noble and decent way - just like a king or queen. Dignity is also about treating yourself and others with pride and respect, like feeling good about who you are. It's like wanting to avoid doing things that might make someone feel embarrassed or not good about themselves. Dignity is all about being proud of yourself and others, and treating everyone with kindness and respect, like a true friend.

Examples:

Dignity is a special quality that every human has, and it means that you deserve to be treated with respect and kindness. It's like having a big, invisible sign that shows others how valuable and important you are.

- The state or quality of being worthy of honor and respect.
- The state of inner posture and attitude.
- Behaving and acting with kindness, decency.
- A desire to avoid doing something that will make another person undignified.
- A sense of modest pride in oneself and others.
- A sense of self-respect, self-esteem, self-worth.
- To neither subordinate nor superordinate, meaning that you don't feel better than others and also don't think that others are better than you.
- Behaving and acting in a way that allows everyone to feel good about themselves.
- Respecting everyone's culture, beliefs, and things they own, just like you want them to respect yours.
- Understanding that everyone needs personal time and space, including you and your friends
- Treating yourself with respect too, and be proud of who you are.
- Respect for dignity and honor excludes any humiliation and degradation.

6.

HOW TO 5+2

Did you notice?

When you look at the 5 definitions throughout the last few chapters in this book so far you can see a hidden word. You can find that special word by looking at the five words in a different way. Are you curious? Have a look. Can you see the word?

Consideration
Admiration
Respect
Empathy
Dignity

Hint: What are the initials of each word? What word can you see when you look at the first letter of each word and read them from top to bottom?

Consideration
Admiration
Respect
Empathy
Dignity

When you take the first letter of each word and read them from the top to the bottom you see a word: <u>Cared</u>! When you start observing the humans around you and measure how they display each of these values you gain a good picture of who they are.

Time is our friend and a good measurement as well. Some people can show how nice they are for a minute, others for a week and longer. I like to observe for 90 days. Does that seem like much time? Some of my famous teachers agree that some people can wear a personality mask for 90 days before we can see who they truly are.

Sun
Mon
Tue
Wed
Thu
Fri
Sat

Have you ever had popcorn when you watched a movie? Did you ever see popcorn pop? When you observe humans around you they too will pop and show who they are over time. Please do not heat up people :-)

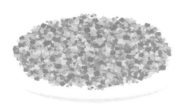

I humbly share with you what works for me:
- Observe behavior
- Watch the show
- Be patient, wait and see
- Staying true to yourself when observing others not behaving according to the 5+2 formula.

No one feels what you feel. No one knows you better than you do. For these reasons it is healthy to protect yourself and your feelings. Not out of fear but out of pro-activity. Being pro-active means that we prepare ourselves and are equipped to meet with humans from all walks of life. Everyone is responsible for their own behavior. If others are unkind, you can remain true to yourself and your standard according to the 5+2 formula.

> **"It is with love as
> it is with plants:
> Who wants to reap love must sow love."**
> Jerimias Gotthelf

Albert Bitzius (October 4, 1797 – October 22, 1854) was a Swiss novelist,
best known by his pen name of Jeremias Gotthelf.

Whatever you feed your mind will grow.
"Wherever your focus goes everything grows.

Reminder: You are the most important human in your life. When you apply the 5+2 on yourself you become your own best friend. This is very attractive to those who also are their own best friend. When two best friends come together so much is possible.

Your thoughts are super powerful! They can make things happen in your mind and body. Your body and mind are <u>always connected</u> with one another. When you have a good thought, your brain releases chemicals that make you feel happy and ready to do things. You feel this in our body and those are called emotions.

E-motions: energy in motion.

So, thinking positively and being kind to ourselves and others can make all relationships and lives better! It's like magic in the brain that helps you feel good. Most importantly, it makes you feel good <u>about yourself.</u>

Sadly, at times humans say things that can make you believe that you are not enough. This is not true! **You are enough! You are ok!** Also, sometimes you may be told to be nice and kind to others without questioning their behavior. It lays in your power to observe other humans and then decide how closely you want to be with them. Sure, it is possible that family members are upset and behave in unloving ways at times. It is important that you keep in mind how worthy you are. You deserve to be treated with consideration, admiration, respect, empathy and dignity.

Consideration
Admiration
Respect
Empathy
Dignity

Who do you give your kindness to? Who do you give small gifts at times? It is a good idea to observe the receiver and how they act and behave with us and those around us. The receiver's actions and behavior tells a lot about them!

When you choose friends and acquaintances based on their **5+2** behavior chances are that you choose well.

Even if you choose carefully who you get closer with, you can still give your kindness to everyone at first. No human being is perfect. We can enjoy each other despite our imperfections, be respectful to each other and be kind and decent. When you are true to yourself and leave others in their own full responsibility regarding their behavior, it is easier not to take things personally. Everyone behaves according to their own standards. So why should I give up or neglect mine? Say "yes" to yourself and your standards even if others have different benchmarks.

7.

THE +2

THE +2

It is time to look at the +2 and what it stands for. The following two points make the **5+2** complete.

Now that you know how to define 5 points out of the **5+2** formula chances are that you allow people closer to your inner world **only** when they live with and display these qualities on a daily basis. When you choose friends and acquaintances based on their **5+2** behavior chances are that you choose well. This helps your heart, your feelings, and your inner world from getting hurt.

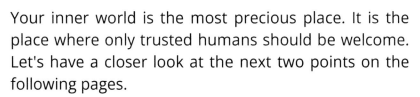

Your inner world is the most precious place. It is the place where only trusted humans should be welcome. Let's have a closer look at the next two points on the following pages.

6. (1st of the +2)

word

wərd/

noun

A word is a meaningful element we use to talk, read, and write. In the 5+2 the word refers to:

- **having** a word
- **keeping** one's word

Meaning of word

Keeping your *word* means doing what you promised or said you would do. Here are some examples:

- To actually do and/or execute what you say you will do.
- Understanding the effect your word has on others.
- Being reliable, accountable, dependable.
- Ability to gain trustworthiness as a result of keeping your word.

6. (1st of the +2)
word
wərd/

noun

- Recreation Promise: If you tell your friend that you'll meet them after lunch, you make sure to go there because you keep your word.
- Sharing things: If you promise to let your sibling or friend borrow something, you do it because you're keeping your word.
- Homework Help: If you say you'll help your classmate with their math homework you make sure to help them like you said.
- Pet Care: If you promise to feed your pet dog every morning, you remember to do it because you want to keep your word.
- Invitation: If you invite your friends to your party on Saturday, you make sure everything is ready for them because you're keeping your word.
- Cleaning Up: If you promise to clean up your room before bedtime, you do it because you're keeping your word.

Keeping your word is important because it shows that you're trustworthy and that people can believe what you say. It shows that you are responsible and reliable. When you can't keep your word or change your mind, inform everyone involved as early as possible. This way others can adjust to the circumstances. It is okay to change your mind.

7. (2nd of the +2)

time·ly
ˈtīmlē/

Timely means doing something at just the right time. It's like arriving at school before the bell rings or finishing your dinner before it gets too late. When you do things timely, it helps everything work smoothly.

man·ner
ˈmanər/

Manner means the way you do something. It's like how you talk, how you eat and how you act. Using good manners also means being polite, using nice words, and being respectful to others. It's like being kind and allowing people feel comfortable when you're around.

time·ly man·ner

'tīmlē/ 'manər/

Doing something in a **timely manner** means doing it at the right time, when it's needed or agreed upon. It's like finishing your homework before dinner, so you have time to play. Or cleaning up your toys right after you're done playing. Doing things in a timely manner helps everything go smoothly and keeps things organized. It helps you have a good conscience. Doing things in a timely manner can help with sleeping well because you know that you did what needed to get done.

Examples:

- Morning routine: Getting dressed, brushing your teeth, and having breakfast before it's time to leave the house or get ready for learning.
- Homework time: Starting your homework as soon as you can, so you have enough time to finish it before dinner.
- Bedtime: Going to bed when you are asked to, so you get enough sleep and wake up refreshed.
- Getting ready: Putting on your shoes and coat when it's time to go out, so you're on time for an outing or activity.
- Let others join in: Take turns with your friends so everyone has a chance to join in and have fun.
- Turning off the TV: Stopping your TV show or video game when you are told it's time, so you can do other important things too.

- Finishing a snack: Eating your snack before it's time for the next activity, like starting your homework or going to the park.
- Cleaning up: Putting away your things after using them, so your room stays organized.
- Arriving at a party: Showing up on time for a friend's party so you don't miss any of the fun activities.
- Getting ready for school: Packing your school bag the night before so you're all set and not rushing in the morning.

Doing things in a timely manner means being aware of the right time to do something and making sure you're ready and prepared. It helps things go smoothly and makes sure everyone has a good time!

It can happen that you are not on time. If you realize you can't do something in a timely manner or change your mind, inform everyone involved so they can adjust to the circumstances.

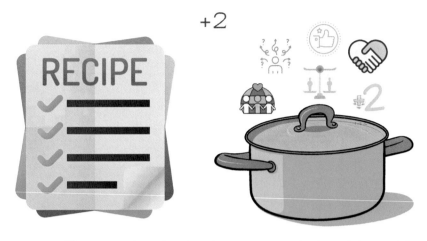

5+2 is like a recipe for having great relationships with people like family and friends. The 5+2 formula is about five important things you can always do and two extra things that are also really important.

Imagine a world where everyone follows the 5+2. Humans treat each other with kindness and respect. They use kind words, talk nicely and make an effort to understand each other's feelings. They help each other and share things. They also remember to be patient and understanding when things are a bit tricky or uneasy.

Now, think about what happens when everyone uses the 5+2 every day. People will be happy, and families, friends, and you feel really good. When everyone follows the **5+2** they get a wonderful reward. The reward is having strong, happy relationships where everyone gets along and cares for each other. The 5+2 doesn't just work with others – it also helps you having a good relationship with yourself!

Everyone Wins

The "prize" or reward you get from using the **5+2** formula is having lots of happiness, love, and strong relationships with others. It's like having a magical way to make the world a better and happier place for everyone. When we always follow the 5+2 formula in our relationships, the special thing we earn is called "trust." Trust is like having a promise that people believe in. It means they know we will do what we say and treat them kindly. When we use the 5+2 formula every day, people will trust us and our relationships become even stronger and happier. It's like a golden prize we get for being kind and respectful to others!

8.

WHO AM I TO WRITE THIS BOOK?

My name is Daisy Papp and I am how I behave. **I love humans.**

I was born and raised in Germany. My life was very challenging at times when I was a child and teenager. It is my passion to support you and show you what is logical, easy-to-understand, and what works wherever you live and whatever your circumstances are. It is fact that you are alive and deserve a life worthwhile living. People in currently 97 countries consider me living proof that it is possible to turn challenges into stepping stones that lead to a joyful life with meaning and passion filled with loving, trusting relationships.

I am the mother of one son. It is my joy to write books and produce a weekly podcast show. My passion is helping humans from around the world to make their lives better and happier. I work with humans from all walks of life and I speak to big audiences about how to achieve a content life. Together we make this world a better place. For you, for me, for everyone, including future generations.

ENDORSEMENTS

ENDORSEMENTS

"5+2 - a fundamental tool in our children's lives."

I thank Daisy from the bottom of my heart for her trust in letting me read this wonderful book in advance.

As a mother of three children, I became instantly aware that the so lovingly described and explained 5+2 method here is a fundamental tool in our children's lives.

We live in a society that is becoming increasingly fast-paced, emotionally colder, and harder to manage. The possibilities, but also the dangers in which changing family structures threaten to take away more and more often the secure hold of the children, seem endless. In such a society it becomes essential that young humans recognize their own value, the value of others, and that all live their dignity.

As a teacher with many years of professional experience, it once again was also made very clear to me that many things are taught and learned in school that children will never need later on. The things that they would actually need for their lives are hardly ever, if at all, addressed in school.

With this book, Daisy Papp does a great job of helping to bridge those gaps. It is written for young humans to show them how easy it can be to live a content, happy and dignified life.

ENDORSEMENTS

The book's title "5+2" had made me curious even before I read the first lines. What looks like a very simple mathematical equation at first that any elementary school student can solve with ease turns out to be actually a complex principle that will have great effects as soon as it is implemented. Like the simple math task, even the youngest children can understand this as soon as they feel how good it is for them and their environment - especially when it is lived and modeled for them.

For this reason, I would like to recommend this book to you first, dear parents. Try the 5+2 method in your family and read the book together with your younger children. Demonstrate the 5+2 formula to your children. Teach your children what the school forgot or what there was simply no time for.

I also recommend this book to older children or young adults. If you feel that certain people are not good for you, if the relationship with friends or relationships just doesn't feel right or real, this book can be a wonderful help to find your way, to realize your real value and to live a happy, satisfied life.

Last but not least, I would also like to recommend Daisy's book of the 5+2 method to my profession, to teachers, but also to educators. The latter because you work at the grassroots level and the youngest children can learn so much from you.

ENDORSEMENTS

If our youngest children already get the opportunity to experience what the 5+2 method feels like, it will become easier and easier, because the even younger, future generations would be born into this loving basic attitude.

Teachers and their students can also benefit from this book. After all, even if the learning schedule seems too little in terms of the overwhelming mass of curriculum content, there are always ways and means to give children a glimpse of Daisy's 5+2- method also in the context of school. Class teacher lessons, Lions Quest lessons or workshops would offer themselves here.

I look forward to the better world we will all create together like this.

Susanne Kramps
Senior Student Councilor and teacher at a grammar school with boarding school in Germany
Subjects: Biology, Geography, Mathematics
Multiple class leader of grades 5-7 (ages 10-12)
Teaching grades 5-13 (ages: 10-18)

ENDORSEMENTS

"Easily digestible treasure trove of Life Lessons for teenagers."

I am enthusiastic about endorsing Daisy Papp's 5+2 Teenager Book. This exceptional guide serves as a guiding light of hope and insight for teenagers as they navigate the intricate terrain of our world. Daisy's profound wisdom shines brilliantly through her compassionate approach, equipping young readers with the necessary tools to embark on a transformative journey of self-discovery and the cultivation of positive relationships. She places a strong emphasis on nurturing one's inner world and making discerning choices in friendships and associations based on the 5+2 values that lead to a state of being 'CARED for.'

As a leader fully committed to the welfare of children and teenagers, I am acutely aware of the profound and lasting impact that early education and guidance can have on their lives. Daisy's book is a wellspring of pragmatic counsel that encourages a heightened awareness of the language we employ, underscores the importance of honoring our commitments, and underscores the value of timeliness in our actions.

In the context of today's divided world, the teaching of these foundational values takes on an unprecedented significance.

ENDORSEMENTS

Daisy's work artfully illuminates the juxtaposition between the innocence of early childhood and the learned behaviors imposed by society, which can leave enduring scars on our hearts. It reinforces the notion that there is no more opportune moment to instill these fundamental values and principles than during the formative years of childhood and adolescence.

As a parent to four children and a dedicated professional in this field, I wholeheartedly extend my endorsement to this easily digestible treasure trove of Life Lessons for teenagers.

Benjamin Kemmer
CEO Florida Keys Children's Shelter

ENDORSEMENTS

"Indispensable guide for teenagers"

Daisy's brilliant, humane teenager book helps the awakening individual who is ready to make his or her way in our divided world.

It is an invitation to work on one's inner world and proactively learn how to choose friends and acquaintances based on the 5+2 values that lead to being CARED. Daisy's common sense guides you to become aware of the words we use, keeping our own word, and doing things in a timely manner. This book points out the basic rules that we should all apply in our everyday relationships.

Daisy contrasts the education in infancy with the learned behavior dictated by society that can leave wounds in our hearts. There is no better time to learn basic values and rules than the CHILD and teenage years!

As a mother, grandmother of four, and doctor, I wholeheartedly recommend this easy-to-read *Pearl of Life Lesson* to all.

Dr. Zsuzsanna Verebelyi Seybold MD
Yale University Preventive Medicine graduate. Enrolled in Barbara Brennan Science Healing

ENDORSEMENTS

"Daisy is exceptionally driven and radiates a passionate commitment to humanity, especially our youth and children worldwide."

Daisy's remarkable journey in healing humans around the world has given her an invaluable ability to connect with individuals who carry deep-seated traumas, both major and minor, accumulated over their lifetimes. Daisy helps unearth these roots and offers an easily accessible toolkit for healing once and for all, enabling individuals to achieve freedom and live with a sense of lightness.

In this book, you will discover seedlings of knowledge and wisdom cultivated from the heart of someone who genuinely comprehends and cares about the betterment of all. Daisy shares what she wishes she had known as a young girl, aiming to assist future generations in finding a smoother path forward. Daisy has developed easily adoptable principles using her '5+2 formula,' which identifies five qualities, plus two more, that one possesses who is genuinely there for you.

Understanding what love is and how to both receive and share it are crucial elements of our human experience. Youth who reads this book will easily relate to and learn how to be an authentic and good friend, while also discovering how to discern whether someone is truly there for them — a vital skill in navigating friendships.

ENDORSEMENTS

Embracing the 5+2 principles will benefit individuals of all ages by sparing them from avoidable heartache and wasted time in inauthentic relationships.

The best part is that the 5+2 method can be applied to all relationships, including parent-child relationships, to help us routinely hold ourselves and those around us accountable.

I hope all humanity reads this book and adopts the 5+2 principles so that we may all be a beacon of love and light to the world.

Peace and love,

Dianne Newberry
Founder of Little Beatles Clubhouse Pre School and Early Childhood Educator, Alberta Canada

ENDORSEMENTS

"5+2: A foundation is laid to unconditionally accept humans, regardless of age. "

With Daisy's 5+2 formula in a book written especially for teenagers, a foundation is laid for accepting humans unconditionally in their essence, and thus everyone, regardless of age. However, the book is also wonderfully suited for parents, educators and social workers, as it gives them easy access to the above in a helpful way. Unconditional acceptance goes hand in hand with consideration, admiration, respect, empathy and dignity in interacting with everyone. This forms an indispensable foundation for understanding everyone as part of the human family. We can foster enthusiasm and development as a matter of the heart, far from predetermined, constricting frameworks. Where better to start than with the youngest humans on earth, the children!!!

With this foundation begun early in school (and of course also before that in kindergartens and in the family), the way is paved for a world that allows and promotes humanly oriented enthusiasm to unfold and in which everyone not only finds their place that corresponds to their innermost heart's desire, because there is no longer any evaluation, because that is what the term "unconditionally" means. Let us embark on the path to this world with Daisy's book.

Martina Steinbeck
Educator at a vocational college

BONUS

BONUS

Your Inner World

In chapter 7 you read about your inner world. It is the most precious place. It is like the place within you filled with treasures and deserving of being safe. With the **5+2** formula it is easy to reveal humans that are not a good fit for you and also shows clearly who can have admission to your inner world. Humans who behave based on the **5+2** consistently can earn trust. **Reminder:** Without trust we have nothing!

When we surround ourselves with trustworthy humans chances are that they are friendly and don't want to hurt us. Humans do make mistakes. Mistakes are leassons to be learned. No one can promise to never hurt you. Important is that they will not hurt you on purpose.

TRUST

Imagine your inner world being surrounded with solely well-intended humans. Is that a wonderful idea?

wonderful

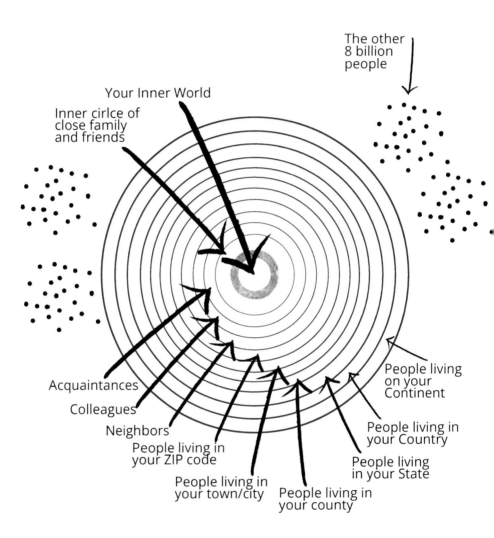

Your Inner World

Inner cirlce of
close family
and friends

The other
8 billion
people

Acquaintances

Colleagues

Neighbors

People living in
your ZIP code

People living in
your town/city

People living in
your county

People living
in your State

People living in
your Country

People living
on your
Continent

BONUS

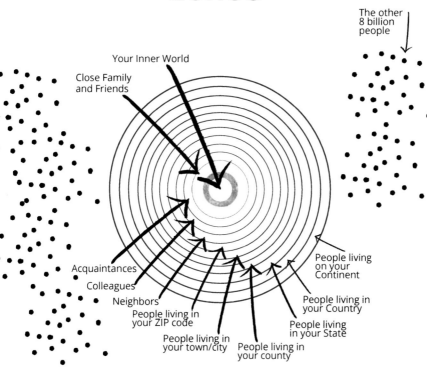

What are the requirements for someone to come close to your inner world? Do you allow humans just randomly enter your inner world by how you feel? Or because they look a certain way? Or because they are good students or have the newest phone?

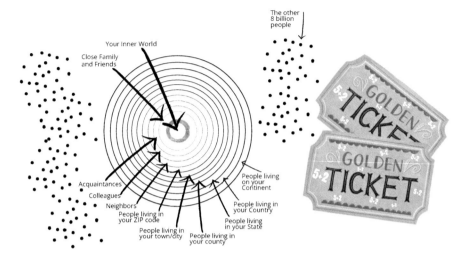

I am very open to meet new people and EVERYONE is welcome into my life! How close someone can come to my inner world depends on their 5+2. Only those who consistently live with the 5+2 formula are allowed into my inner circle.

You matter!

Can you see how your inner world can be a safe place? Enjoy your newly learned 5+2 formula. Share widely and far so our world can be the peaceful paradise it was created to be.

9.

THANK YOU

THANK YOU

Thank you from the bottom of my heart for reading my words. Your persistence reading through the pages of this book is changing the world! Every human who starts living by 5+2 changes the world. Together we are many and together we are strong.

When you have questions please contact me. I am here to support you and your family and friends. Whatever I can do to support making your life better, I will do. I live by the 5+2. Let's meet where the 5+2 is alive every day. I wish you much love!

THANK YOU

Wholeheartedly, I also thank the many helping humans who have lovingly supported me in completing this book: Tian, Birgit, Dianne, Martina, Rob, Susanne, Kathi, Trish, Renee, and many more.

We are many! Together we are strong!

OTHER PUBLICATIONS BY DAISY PAPP

You can find other books by Daisy Papp on the www.daisypapp.com website. All publications by Daisy are teenager friendly. Enjoy!

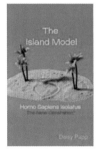

Listen to the Bald and Blonde Mindset Evolution Podcast on your favorite streaming platform. This Podcast is free of explicit language and content.

The show is teenager friendly. Enjoy!
www.baldandblonde.live

When you want to invite Daisy to speak at your event, to your community, school, or organization fill out the contact form here: daisypapp.com/contact

DISCLAIMER

You can read through (or skip) the text in the following paragraphs. It is legal stuff to protect me and my company, so I can continue writing and speak freely about my findings that help you and others. I see it as an important step to be pro-active in life.

This book demonstrates impressive personal improvement tools. It is not a substitute for training in psychology or psychotherapy. The author urges the reader to use these techniques under the supervision of a qualified therapist or physician. The author and publisher does not assume responsibility for how the reader chooses to apply the techniques herein. The ideas, procedures, and suggestions in this book are not intended as a substitute for consultation with your professional health care provider. If you have any questions about whether or not to use EFT or any other of the offered methods in the SelfRecoding© concept, consult your physician or licensed mental health practitioner.

The information in this book is of a general nature only, and may not be used to treat or diagnose any particular disease or any particular person. Reading this book does not constitute a professional relationship or professional advice or services. No endorsement or warranty is explicit or implied by any entity connected to this book, and there is no guarantee that you will have the same results. Further, Daisy Papp is not a licensed health professional and offers the information in this book solely as a life coach.

The information is based on information from sources believed to be accurate and reliable. Every reasonable effort has been made to present the shared information as complete and accurate as possible and most information and tools in this book are based on research and scientific study, but such completeness and accuracy cannot be guaranteed and is not guaranteed.

Neither the author, publisher, SelfRecoding©, and contributors to this book, nor their successors, assigns, licenses, employees, officers, directors, attorneys, agents, and other parties related to them (a) do not make any representations, warranties, or guarantees that any of the information will produce any particular medical, psychological, physical, mental, or emotional result; (b) are not engaged in the rendering of medical, psychological, or other advice or services; (c) do not provide diagnosis, care, treatment, or rehabilitation of any individual; and (d) do not necessarily share the views and opinions expressed in the information.

The information has not undergone evaluation and testing by the United States Food and Drug Administration or similar agency of any other country and is not intended to diagnose, treat, prevent, mitigate, cure, or heal any disease. Risks that might be determined by such testing are unknown. If the reader purchases any services or products as a result of the information, the reader or user acknowledges that the reader or user has done so with informed consent. The information is provided on an "as is" basis without any warranties of any kind, express or implied, whether warranties as to use, merchantability, fitness for a particular purpose, or otherwise.

The author, publisher, SelfRecoding©, and contributors to this book, nor their successors, assigns, licenses, employees, officers, directors, attorneys, agents, and other parties related to them (a) expressly disclaim any liability for and shall not be liable for any loss or damage including but not limited to use of the information; (b) shall not be liable for any direct or indirect compensatory, special, incidental, or consequential damages or costs of any kind or character; (c) shall not be responsible for any acts or omissions by any party including but not limited to any party mentioned or included in the information or otherwise; (d) do not endorse or support any material or information from any party mentioned or included in the information or otherwise; and (e) will not be liable for damages or costs resulting from any claim whatsoever.

Made in the USA
Las Vegas, NV
21 December 2023

83370940R00055